This book is due for return on or before the last date shown below.

D1429328

More Praise for
I HAVE A STRATEGY
(NO YOU DON'T)

"Finally, a book that strips away the jargon, dispels the myths, and dispenses with endless hours of consultant-led meetings. It's like having a secret strategy weapon. With characteristic wit and intelligence, Malham tells us where most strategic planning processes go wrong—and how we can get it right. A must for anyone searching for a clear path to a winning strategy."

—**Steve Edwards**, deputy director of programming, University of Chicago's Institute of Politics

"A smart, entertaining, and interesting read. I'd recommend it to anybody, in any field, who wants to know the elements of strategy and how to apply them."

—**Greg Parsons**, vice president, Herman Miller

I HAVE A STRATEGY
(NO YOU DON'T)

I HAVE A STRATEGY
(NO YOU DON'T)

THE ILLUSTRATED GUIDE TO **STRATEGY**

WRITTEN AND ILLUSTRATED BY

HOWELL J. MALHAM JR.

Foreword by Jeff Leitner

JOSSEY-BASS
A Wiley Imprint
www.josseybass.com

Published by Jossey-Bass
A Wiley Imprint
One Montgomery Street, Suite 1200, San Francisco, CA 94104-4594—www.josseybass.com

Library of Congress Cataloging-in-Publication Data

Malham Jr., Howell J.
  I have a strategy (no you don't) : the illustrated guide to strategy / Howell J. Malham, Jr. -- 1st ed.
      p. cm.
  Includes bibliographical references.
  ISBN 978-1-118-48420-3 (cloth); ISBN 978-1-118-52659-0 (ebk.); ISBN 978-1-118-52631-6 (ebk.);
ISBN 978-1-118-52644-6 (ebk.)
  1. Strategic planning. I. Title.
  HD30.28.M333 2013
  658.4'012--dc23

                                                                    2012038508

Printed in the United States of America
FIRST EDITION

HB Printing 10 9 8 7 6 5 4 3 2 1

CONTENTS

For Ralph

You keep using that word. I do not think it means what you think it means.

—*The Princess Bride (1987)*

Strategy is not like love.

It isn't ethereal, subjective, or hard to define.

It is concrete, specific, and was defined in approximately the same way for centuries across virtually all cultures. Then, somehow, it got fuzzy. And now, far too often, it has come to mean a whole host of things that aren't strategy.

I have no idea how this happened. But this matters a lot.

Generally, it matters because definitions matter. In constructing buildings, crossbeams are crossbeams and aren't floorboards or drywall. In performing surgery, scalpels are scalpels and aren't sponges or forceps.

Specifically, it matters because Howell and I depend on it to do our jobs. As founders of Insight Labs—think of it as research and development for social change—we design new models for saving the world. But we don't always build out those models ourselves; sometimes, we turn over our designs to other people who don't really understand what strategy is, much less how to use strategy to realize big ideas.

So we give them designs and they produce far, far less than they could.

This book is Howell's remarkable effort to fix production. It was born of yet another meeting with corporate executives spouting verbiage and offering suggestions they thought were strategy but sadly weren't. His response that day was the first draft of this wonderful book.

Believe me—nothing beats Howell delivering this lesson in person. But this book comes damn close. Enjoy and, in the event we collaborate down the road, please pay attention.

—Jeff Leitner, founder and dean, Insight Labs

ACKNOWLEDGMENTS

I grew up in a family that loved words.

We loved debating their meanings and pronunciations at the dinner table; we loved discovering and learning their etymologies; we loved using and sharing new and "big" words with one another, sometimes just to show off in front of Mom and Dad.

As the youngest of seven kids, I was at a disadvantage for a few years. My older brothers and sisters were busy building their vocabularies long before I showed up on planet Earth. Sometimes, they used strange and exotic words at the table that left me dumbfounded. Whenever I'd ask, "What does *that* mean?" I was encouraged to excuse myself and look up the word in the massive *Webster's International Dictionary* on the wooden stand in my father's study.

I hated those trips at first. The family dinner conversation would continue downstairs, while I prowled around the dictionary for some word I could barely pronounce, let alone spell. Inevitably, while searching for one definition, I would become dizzily distracted by other entries, some with curious illustrations, and end up running down and reading about words I wasn't even looking for.

This book is a story about one of those words.

It's not a long, or terribly elegant word, one of those sesquipedalian delights. It's a simple and very common word that is overused and frequently, tragically misunderstood.

Yes. There are worse crimes than using a word incorrectly, but not many. For me, there is nothing more important than understanding the words we use to communicate the thoughts and ideas we have—especially when we're communicating with one another. It's how civilization became, well, *civilized*.

One person may say *tom-a-to*, the other may say *tom-ah-to*—but woe if one of those people believes *tomato* really means *shoehorn*. Or worse.

It will, of course, require more than one word to thank the many brilliant and big-hearted folks in my sphere who made this exposition on strategy possible—some, I'm not embarrassed to say, who are far more learned than I am on this subject.

Many thanks are due straightaway to my mom and dad, from whom I inherited this endless and sometimes vexing fascination with words. And I'm grateful as always to my brothers and sisters, my extended family, and my friends for their encouragement, inspiration, and guidance throughout the years.

I owe a debt of gratitude to my colleague and friend, Jeff Leitner. He challenged my preconceived notions of "strategy" and exhorted me to conduct a personal, unapologetic analysis of the word in order to discover and transmit its whatness. I also thank Andrew Benedict-Nelson, another colleague and friend, who offered scholarly advice, direction, and more than a few thoughtful comments on the manuscript.

Dr. Robert Wolcott, Jim Newcomb, Deepa Gupta, Slava Rubin, Sarah Elizabeth Ippel, Melinda Tuan, Bill Sleeth, Mark Trammell, Ann Hill, and many others provided invaluable insight on strategy in their respective realms. Marnie Breen Vosper, Bryan Campen, and Maggie Hendrie gave their time and talents, helping me negotiate hurdles during the early stages of writing this book. And, at a critical moment, Kelli Christiansen helped me to realize the full potential of the project and encouraged me to press on. Try as I may, I cannot thank them enough.

I'm deeply grateful to Jim and Dawn Jacoby for their friendship, enthusiasm, and tireless support. And to Ashima Dayal and Ryann Whalen for much-needed, on-the-spot counsel. I'm equally indebted to Aaron Schoenherr and Lisa Seidenberg at Greentarget. They're fearless evangelists whose collective belief has enlarged and deepened the importance of this and other Insight Labs projects.

Many others helped see this book through to completion, namely Adrian Morgan, art director; Rob Brandt, editorial projects manager; and Kelsey McGee, senior production editor, who talked me down from the ledge more than once with kindness, patience, and wisdom. I thank them one and all.

Special thanks indeed are due to my agent Jeffrey Krames and my editor Susan Williams at Jossey-Bass, who believed when others doubted. And for that I'm eternally grateful.

I offer these final words of thanks and praise to my wife Cheryl, who read draft after draft, saved me from silly errors, made thousands of brilliant suggestions, and not the least, tolerated the febrile, fanatical antics of a man on deadline.

I HAVE A STRATEGY
(NO YOU DON'T)

Strategy.

It's an interesting word, isn't it?

If you say it over and over, it starts to sound really strange.

(Try it.)

Strategy. Strategy. Strategy. Strategy. Strategy.
Strategy. Strategy. Strategy. Strategy. Strategy.
 Strategy. Strategy. Strategy. Strategy. Strategy.
Strategy. Strategy. Strategy. Strategy. Strategy.
Strategy. Strategy. Strategy. Strategy. Strategy.
Strategy. Strategy. Strategy. Strategy. Strategy.
Strategy. Strategy. Strategy. Stra . . . Strate . . . Str . . .

It's a military term derived from the Greek word στρατηγία (*stratēgia*) meaning "generalship" or "the art of the general."

Sun Tzu—the great Chinese general who authored *The Art of War* more than two thousand years ago—gave a great deal of thought to strategy.

He said, "All men can see these tactics whereby I conquer, but what none can see is the strategy out of which victory is evolved."

If you can't see something, does it exist?

—Yes. I can't see my rubber ball because it is behind our sofa. It still exists. It's just hidden by the sofa. Gosh, I love that ball.

Can you love something even if you can't see it?

—Yes. I love my rubber ball, even though I can't see it right now.

What if the ball didn't really exist? Would you still love it?

—If something doesn't exist, why even bother talking about it?

Good point! Will you give the keynote at the Atheist Alliance dinner?

—No.

Carl von Clausewitz thought a lot about it, too.

He was a Prussian military strategist who fought against Napoleon Bonaparte I, emperor of the French.

In his famous book, *On War*, Clausewitz defined strategy as "the use of engagements for the object of war."

There he is, Gary! It's Napoleon! He's attacking!

—No he's not, Larry! He's retreating!

Which is it??

—I don't know!

Wow. He IS good.

These days, you hear the word *strategy* in business. You hear it *a lot*.

We need a strategy, Gary!

Strategy, strategy, strategy

Strategy, strategy, strategy

Strateg, strat . . . , stra . . .

Problem is, most people in business don't know what it means.

Listen to me, Gary.

—Why should I listen to you?

I have an MBA, Gary.

—What does that mean?

It's proof that I paid for a degree to learn about stuff that will help me build a company for the last century.

—Oh. Well, wouldn't you rather use your mind to create new knowledge? That's more important than learning.

That sounds too hard. I'd rather examine your EBITDA.

—I should probably let my doctor do that.

You're right. Where is your EBITDA located, anyway?

—My upper or lower EBITDA?

Never mind.

Most people confuse a strategy with a tactic. That's a very common mistake.

Okay, Gary, here's the strategy. Now, listen up:
We're going to blast people with billions of emails!
Emails with LINKS! Lots and lots of
embedded LINKS! You got me?

      —Okay. What are we emailing them?

It doesn't matter! Just email them!
And make sure you include links.
Lots and lots of links!

      —You live a confusing life.

A single tactic is *not* a strategy.

People who believe that are confused.

My father would encourage all of us to "pray for them."

And please, PLEASE help Larry understand that a strategy is not a tactic, Amen. . . .

Some think strategy is a tool. That's another mistake.

Listen to me, Gary.

I've got a strategy.

It's an app!

For a smart phone!

—Great! What does it do?

Gary?

—What?

Will you do me a favor?

—What favor?

Will you stop answering
questions with questions?

—I will if YOU stop asking ME
questions that YOU don't
want answered.

Fine.

They're confused, too.

Or they never had an opportunity to learn about strategy.

Or they're just lazy.

We pray for them as well.

(We pray they go away.)

Others think strategy is visual design.

Okay, Gary. Here's the web strategy:
Make the BUY button REALLY big.
I mean REALLY big. I'm talking a great
big BUY button. Bigger than the actual page!
And change the copy to "BUY NOW." And add an
exclamation mark! No! On second thought, spell out
the exclamation mark! Are you with me?
Are you with me, Gary?

Those people are very creative.

And have a really good eye.

And may very well understand the principles of design.

But graphic design alone is not a strategy.

—What will compel people to visit our
website in the first place, Larry?
And what's going to make them come
back to our site over and over?
What's going to make them trust and
believe in our site? How do we win their allegiance AND
devotion FOREVER?
Huh, Larry?

A big, personalized "BUY NOW" button!
That's how! AND they'll get to choose
their OWN colors for the button, too!
They love that!

Here's the simplest way to define *strategy*:

A planned, *doable* sequence of actions designed to achieve a distinct, measurable goal.

Hmmm. Is a strategy a strategy if
you don't have the power to execute it?

—I don't think so.

What is it, then?

—A fairy tale.

What's a fairy tale?

—An implausible dream.

What makes it implausible?

—An ending that has absolutely no relationship
to reality.

Oh. I prefer happy endings.

—Then you should stick to American
cinema.

That's it.

Pretty simple, really. (But simple isn't easy.)

From this point on, promise yourself you will *never* take another meeting to discuss strategy until everybody *in* the meeting is clear on the definition of "strategy."

(It will be a better meeting, I promise.)

—A common language is very important if we're going to work together!

Yes, but what do YOU mean by "important"?"

—What do you mean?

Well, what do YOU mean by "mean"?

—What are you talking about?

Well, what do YOU mean by "YOU"?

—Are you billing for this?

What do YOU mean by "this"?

—If you ask me another question, I'm not paying you.

Fine.

Spending time and money in meetings to develop a strategy without a distinct, measurable goal is not smart.

(By the way, it's not strategizing either.)

It's called something else.

It's called f#@king off.

On company time.

(There's a lot of that going around these days.)

I Have a Strategy (No You Don't)

Business is full of "strategists" who don't know how to strategize, developing strategies for clients who don't know what *strategy* means.

After months and months, and hours and hours, self-proclaimed "strategists" deliver a big, fat PowerPoint with lots of charts and graphs. And then present very large bills.

—Is THIS my strategy, Larry?

If by "strategy" you mean a PowerPoint, then, yes, it's your strategy, Gary.

—Wait a minute! This looks like the last PowerPoint, er, strategy you showed me.

Uh-uh. Last time, I used the converging arrows graphic. THIS time, I used the DIVERGING arrows graphic!

—Oh. That IS different. And definitely worth all the money I'm about to pay you.

What do you mean by "all"?

—Are we going to start that again?

Those folks are not really strategists. They're time wasters. Worse—
you *now* think you have a strategy when you don't. (Remember *The
Emperor's New Clothes?*)

Let's go somewhere and do something, Gary!
Here's how I propose we do it
and here are the tactics we're going to use
to do what I propose to do, Gary!

—Okay! That's sounds like a strategy!
Where are we going?

I don't know.

—Why do we want to go THERE?

Not sure.

—So. You don't know where we're going,
or why, but you're going to tell me how
we're going to get there?

Yes.

—Um. That doesn't sound right.

Be quiet. I have an MBA.

So, when is a strategy really a strategy?

I Have a Strategy (No You Don't)

A strategy is a strategy if:

1. It has an intended purpose.

Hey, Gary, I was working on a strategy to put a cookie back in the cookie jar but I tripped and fell and the cookie flew into my mouth instead. Good strategy, huh?

—That's not a strategy.
  That's a happy accident, Larry.

It's not an accident
that I'm happy, is it?

—Not if you took your
medication.

A strategy is a strategy if:

2.   There is a plan.

Strategies happen in the future,
not in the past, Gary.

—In retrospect, I believe you.

I Have a Strategy (No You Don't)

A strategy is a strategy if:

3. There is a sequence of actions.

If Tinker throws the ball to Evers, and Evers throws the ball to Chance, we'll have a double play. . . .

—Yes, but they played for the Cubs and that team might not win a World Series for hundreds of years.

Yeah, but who's counting?

—Not the fans, obviously.

Obviously. They keep showing up.

—Well, if they finally win a World Series, they won't be so special anymore. And people may stop showing up, even though they have a really cute, old-fashioned stadium.

You're right! If they end their historic losing streak, they'd lose their one market differentiator! So maybe they're playing to lose! What a strategy!

—That's not strategy. That's bad baseball.

A strategy is a strategy if:

4. There is a distinct, measurable goal.

You can't count it if you don't know what IT is.

—And if you can't count it, IT
doesn't count!

But we can still BILL
for it, right?

—I think so.

Phew! Billing
means the
world to me.

Those are the elements of strategy.

Let's recap. A strategy is a strategy *if* it has:

1. A purpose

2. A plan

3. A sequence of actions or tactics

4. A distinct, measurable goal

A strategy isn't a strategy without the power to execute it, Gary!

—Well, even if we don't have the power to make it work NOW, we might be able to make it work LATER.

Later is just a theory, and how empty is a theory in the face of now?

—That's really profound. Did you just make that up? Or did somebody else say that?

I believe Life is the only author.

—Oh. So you DID steal it!

Let's talk about this later.

—Fine.

Every strategy needs at least one, essential tactic—that is, an action or device to help achieve a measurable goal.

It needs a narrative.

The *story*.

It's how to package and sell your strategy.

It's how to create *buy-in* and inspire others to understand, maybe even *love* your strategy.

Without a narrative, you can only sell strategy to strategists, which is like selling chemistry to chemists.

—Here is a molecular model of strategy, Larry.

That doesn't look interesting to me.
But I'm not really a strategist, Gary.

—Hmmm. Maybe it
needs a story to
pull it all together?

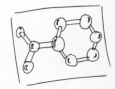

Like a covalent bond?

—Well, more of a
cohesive bond.

It's all relevant.

—You mean relative?

Sure.

Four main elements and one, essential megatactic. That's a strategy.

If strategy were a mathematical equation it might look like this:

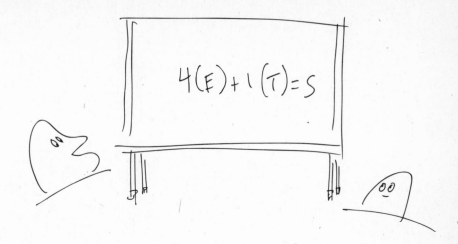

Let's look at strategy in action:

I Have a Strategy (No You Don't)

Like the strategy that parents use to get kids to eat vegetables they don't want to eat.

OKAY, GARY, OPEN UP!
GARY! GARY! GARY!

Combining a sense of play and imagination, parents develop a strategy that magically transforms a fork into an airplane . . . and changes a kid's mouth into an airplane hangar.

Okay, here's the airplane! Remember!
It's not a fork! And that is NOT broccoli!

—How do I know it's not a fork?

Because forks don't make these
kinds of noises! Airplanes do!
Vrrrrrrrrroooooooooom!

—You're not my mom. Stop
feeding me.

Be quiet and play the game.

More than just reframing the value and importance of broccoli, the parent uses a story—narrative—to manipulate the way information about the broccoli is presented and served to the kid.

Dinner is no longer dinner. The broccoli is no longer broccoli.

Dinner is a game: Put the airplane—and its cargo—in the airplane hangar.

It's a positive experience that *inspires* kids to play along. Eagerly.
Happily. For their own pleasure.

Inspiration is the mother of belief, Gary!

—I know. One must feel before one believes.

If you're so smart then why are you

asking me all these questions?

—I haven't asked you any questions.

No? Then why are you listening to me?

—My strategy is to allow you to tell me things

I already know so you underestimate my intelligence

and overestimate your own.

To what end?

—You'll tell me everything you know, which usually

isn't very much, and I'll use that information to

control future conversations and count all the times

I get my way.

That's a ruthless strategy. You don't look like
the ruthless type.

—The best cutthroats aren't cutthroats.

I'm calling you Stalin from now on.

—I prefer Uncle Joe.

And it gets kids to do something they don't want to do.

(Like eat vegetables.)

It's a good strategy. And it has all the elements:

. The parent has a *purpose*: Help kid to grow up strong and healthy.

There is a *plan*: Prepare well-balanced dinners *with* vegetables that have minerals and iron.

There is a *sequence of actions*: Plan menu. Boil broccoli. Set table. Play game.

There is a *distinct, measurable goal*: Kid must ingest at least 6.2 pieces of *broccoli*.

And a narrative. The *story*:

Vrooooooom!
Vrrooooooom!

I Have a Strategy (No You Don't)

And everybody likes a story. It's in our DNA.

What are you doing, Gary?

—I'm trying to develop a strategy to get a community of consumers to eat pork.

Hmmm. Have you tried turning pork on a fork into an airplane?

—No. But I have thought about developing a narrative that includes calling pork "the other white meat."

That sounds racist. I'd try turning pork on a fork into an airplane. It's safer.

—Good idea.

It also created a memorable family experience.

One that can be repeated for generations.

Hey Gary, what do you call it when something can be mass produced and delivered cheaply and efficiently for mass consumption over and over and over and over?

—The surest way to kill a really good idea?

Oh. I thought we called it "scalable."

—That's your MBA talking.

Just make sure you know your audience with this kind of strategy.

And be sure that the kid is just being bratty and uncooperative if he says he doesn't want to eat broccoli.

And that he doesn't have a food allergy.

—Uh-oh. I think I'm going to be sick, Larry.

You're fine, Gary.

—No. I told you I can't eat broccoli, Larry.

You CAN'T eat it?
Or you don't WANT to eat it?

—Can't.

Now you tell me.

Here's another example.

The United States once used a diplomatic strategy as part of a bigger plan to prevent the Soviet Union from taking over the world.

The strategy even had a name:

Containment.

The United States developed a very convincing narrative that referred to Soviet communism as some kind of venereal disease, not an economic system. So, the free world (that is, the "uncontaminated") worked like the dickens to "quarantine" communist states to prevent the spread of "the sickness."

You're sick, Comrade Gary. And you're NOT to leave the red zone.

—But my doctor says YOU'RE the sick one, Comrade Larry, and I'M the healthy one.

That's because your doctor is sick, too! Remember, it's not the thermometer that counts; it's the one taking the temperature!

—Well, what if YOUR doctor is the sick one, Comrade Larry?

That's impossible, Comrade Gary.

—How do YOU know, Comrade Larry?

It's HIS thermometer.

—Oh.

It worked . . . for a while.

But when containing the "Commies" required the United States to fight a long and nasty war in Vietnam, the whole thing kinda fell apart.

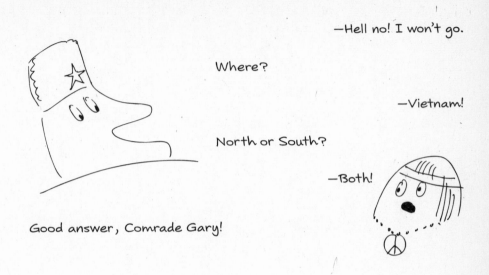

—Hell no! I won't go.

Where?

—Vietnam!

North or South?

—Both!

Good answer, Comrade Gary!

Pretty soon, we realized it was better to try and relax and not get all worked up over communism.

So, we took a "time out." We *relaxed*.

(The French describe this as *détente*. Sounds more elegant than *time out*.)

It allowed the United States to focus on another strategy:

I Have a Strategy (No You Don't)

Accelerated instability.

The United States and the rest of the free world worked to acceler-ate instability within the USSR, exploiting the fact that Gorbachev's "reforms" in the 1980s were making the large, ungainly, and economi-cally backward "superpower" *more* unstable.

One way, but surely not the *only* way, was to keep the Soviets pinned down in a spending war, which helped bring about the need for economic reforms in the first place.

There can be many strategies leading to the same outcome, right?

—Yep. But I think the goal is to find one that is the most relevant, doable, and has the highest chances of success.

Wow. That makes a lot of sense. But I would NEVER admit that to you.

—You just did.

It was a war they couldn't win.

Why?

Because Soviet communists did not know how to make money.

But Western capitalists did.

The more money the West made, the more it invested in defense. And the United States told *that* story, loudly and proudly.

And when the "Commies" tried, among other things, to match the United States on defense, they went broke. (A particularly long and nasty war in Afghanistan didn't help matters for the USSR.)

I think the U.S. helped Jihadists and other insurgents defeat the Soviets in Afghanistan.

—I think you're right.

And I think similar insurgents are now fighting against the U.S. in Afghanistan.

—Me, too.

Have we learned anything from this?

—I think so.

What?

—The only check-out is a late check-out at the Motel Kandahar.

In a matter of time, the Soviet Union caved in on itself.

Okay, Gary! Start building that
"Star Wars" defense system-thingy!

—But the technology doesn't exist yet,
Larry! And this is all a ploy!

No excuse. Get cracking.

More significant, as David Kotz and Fred Weir discovered after interviewing Soviet insiders, a tiny percentage of elite party members—who initially fought to preserve the old, rickety structure and maintain the status quo—suddenly woke up to the fact that they would lose *all* their privileges and power if Gorby had his way.

(They learned this lesson from the clergy and aristocrats in the French Revolution, who thought King Louis XVI's financial reforms were far more threatening to their existence—and the entire social hierarchy, for that matter—than anything on the commoners' wish list, which is why so many of them threw in with the Third Estate.)

Many Soviets also realized that they would benefit *more* if the system, in fact, collapsed.

And it did—*with their help*—under the strain of perestroika.

Quite a successful strategy for the United States, yes?

It had a *purpose*: Win the Cold War.

It had a *plan*: Leverage economic resources, among others, to accelerate the instability of a rival superpower as it struggles to reform.

It had a *sequence of interdependent events*: United States increases defense spending, which causes Soviets to increase defense spending, which means they have less money to produce basic necessities for their own people, which makes the people angry, which puts more pressure on Gorby to call for more reforms, which makes the government even more unstable, which gets insiders rooting and working for a collapse.

It had a *distinct, measurable end*: There are *two* superpowers. Let's make it one.

And it had a *great* narrative:

The Soviets are "The Evil Empire." And they must go. . . .

Problem was, the United States didn't know how to stop spending. And the trade deficit increased. And the debt grew larger.

And America's biggest creditor became the People's Republic of China: *communists*!

Unlike the Soviets, Chinese communists are really, really good at creating wealth and managing it.

(Better than the United States, in fact. They must have learned all their tricks while watching Americans play poker with the Soviets. And win.)

Now the Chinese government has a strategy. Give us enough rope, er, credit, to hang ourselves.

But don't worry. The People's Republic of China would *never* let our economy collapse. They need each of us to have just enough money to buy all those ticky-tacky holiday decorations that they export. (Hence, the trade deficit.)

嗨, Larry!

What??

我说， "嗨, Larry!"

I can't understand you, Gary.

那么你最好尽快学习中文， 因为这已是它们的世界了，

我们只是在这里暂住。

That's it. I'm blocking Google Translate.

你不是我的老板。 中国才是。

There's more than one way to solve a problem with strategy. The trick is knowing the best way to solve the problem.

They say there's a million ways into a strategy but only ONE right way.

—How do you know the right way?

You don't. That's why it's better to have an active, flexible strategy that allows you to manage and course-correct in real time.

—Oh.

And when there's billions and billions of dollars at stake, companies want to make sure they're betting on the right strategy, at the right time.

Sometimes, these strategies compete with one another in the marketplace.

Sometimes they attack.

Take the long-running feud between Boeing and Airbus.

—Doesn't it take like a thirty-year investment to build a new kind of airplane?

Yep. Something like that.

—How can you course-correct when you're locked into a thirty-year investment?

It's not easy. You just need to make sure that you really believe in what you're building, and that your customer will always believe in the values that you believe in, like convenience and comfort.

—AND hope somebody doesn't invent something that ENDS the world of airplanes in the meantime.

Each company in its own way has been trying to develop a strategy to meet repeated demands for "efficiency."

Efficiency! Efficiency! Efficiency! That's all we hear in this industry!

—Lower fares, too. Our customers' customers always want lower fares.

Seems everybody knows the price of everything and the value of nothing!

—Oscar Wilde?

No. Larry.

—Oh! Very nice to meet you!

Pleasure.

Airbus believes the route to efficiency is through bigger, more luxurious planes that offer a variety of up-in-the-air amenities and fly "hub and spoke."

That is, fly superjumbo planes nonstop to central "hub" locations, where passengers connect to other flights on smaller planes and travel along the "spoke" to outlying destinations.

No surprise, then, that Airbus built the biggest superjumbo plane the world has ever seen. The A380. It's big. *Really* big. It's a double-decker and can carry up to 850 passengers.

It has sleeper cabins. It has cocktail lounges. It has fitness clubs.

Wow! This plane is HUGE! It has everything!
It's like a flying hotel!

—Yes, but it's not flying anywhere we want to fly.

Who cares! I have my own bed and a big, fluffy pillow and linens with a really high thread count!
I may never want to leave!
I think I want to live here!
Who do I see about long-term living planes?

—Planes?

I mean plans. Hello, Dr. Freud!

—Press the button marked "Leasing Agent."

A few things to keep in mind about an airline that flies hub and spoke: they need to make sure they have lots of passengers on those big, superjumbo planes, maximizing the number of people going from point A to point B.

Increase the number of people. Increase the profit.

But . . . the bigger the plane is, the harder it is to fill.

Now. If you're comparing on price, airlines with big, superjumbo planes—like the A380—can be wildly competitive *if* they're full.

If you're looking at price *and* convenience *and* time, then it's harder to be competitive, especially if there are other planes that fly point to point in comfort and safety . . . and in a humidity-controlled cabin.

The bet Airbus is making: Airlines will fill the A380 to capacity. And *that's* how they'll make money.

Economies through scale.

But again, there's more risk playing for more volume. Not to mention the headaches of getting different travelers to a hub at the same time to connect.

Every time there's a mistake or a delay, it just doesn't irritate passengers—it hinders an airline's ability to fill the airplane.

And they can't be profitable if they don't have nearly full flights.

—When we plan our next trip, we should plan it based on where jumbo planes fly, not on where we want to go. That way we can enjoy all the great attractions of a luxury liner.

That's silly.

—How SHOULD we plan it, then?

We should plan it based on departures from the nearest gate. I HATE walking to gates that are far away.

—Flights at the first few gates only fly to places like Sacramento or Chattanooga.

Okay, then maybe we should just take a nice, quiet drive to your mother's house?

—Fine. I'll go to Chattanooga.

Think about it: You fly a bunch of people to Tokyo or Cairo or Mumbai. Then make them get off a big, superjumbo plane, and shuttle them to another plane—sometimes with seconds to spare—that will carry them to their final destination.

Boeing must have thought, *People will hate that.*

They believed people might want to go somewhere other than Tokyo or Cairo or Mumbai.

Somewhere like Okinawa.

And they believed that they might want to get there *direct*.

Without the rush or hassle of connecting through a hub.

So they set out to develop a different strategy to solve for efficiency.

It's a strategy that turns on the belief that there is something better, *much* better, than bigger.

Better *technologically*, that is.

While Airbus banked on big, bad luxury liners like the A380 that offer passengers hub and spoke, Boeing bet billions on a smaller, technologically innovative aircraft that gives airlines the opportunity to offer passengers comfort and *plenty* of destination choices:

The B787 Dreamliner.

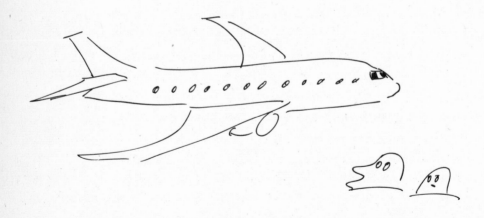

It's a plane that takes people where they want to go. Point to point. *Direct.*

To create the 787, Boeing had to rely on technological smarts that would enable them to take two big issues off the table: fuel cost and distance.

Take fuel and distance off the table, they believed, and it's game over.

Every company wants to "kill" its competition, Gary.

—They do? I thought we're all in this together, Larry?

We are. But companies need to make money to stay in business.

—But can't EVERYBODY make money?

You're not really making money if your competition isn't losing money. It's a zero-sum game: You can't win unless they lose.

—Isn't there a better, saner way to keep score in this life?

I don't know. I just know how to count money.

—And how do you feel about that?

Pretty good. How do I look?

—Terrible.

Phew. That means I'm doing something right.

So they set out to create something lighter and sleeker and more *efficient*.

And reinvented the airplane in the process.

But first, they asked, What do passengers *really* want?

They want to go where they want to go (point to point).

Safely, comfortably, and at a reasonable price.

And a reasonable price, we know, comes from efficiency.

No doubt: It's a more efficient *market* strategy to route traffic through a network hub—efficient for the airlines, but not necessarily the passengers.

It would work, too, if this were the era of the 747, and there were no other planes like it that can fly passengers to exotic hubs far and away.

We missed the connecting flight, Gary!
That's it! I'm never flying this airline again!

    —Write an indignant letter to the CEO.

What good will THAT do?

—He might feel bad and send you a free ticket.

What am I going to do with a free ticket for a flight on an airline that I never want to fly again?

—Okay. Then write a letter to *The Times*.

What good will THAT do?

    —The CEO of the airline might read the letter in the morning paper and send you a free ticket.

But I told you, I don't WANT a free ticket!

    —How about a pair of plastic wings and a stack of drink tickets?

Deal.

It's not so great if there are other equally comfy, more fuel-efficient planes that competitors can fly to the same exotic locations, and many, many other points on the map.

A plane like the B787.

Let's face it: *All* airlines want passengers to be happy, and they want people to fly with them, and they want to make money.

They also want to give passengers a sense of safety and security.

Passengers will be perfectly safe flying on either the A380 or the B787.

But what will make them extra *happy*?

A. Flying nonstop to Chicago to Dubai for $1,500?

Or,

B. Flying Chicago to London to Dubai for $1,500?

The B787 can get them to Dubai direct—a remarkable engineering feat for such an aircraft.

The A380 might not fly direct, but it offers more luxury perks in the sky, like cocktail lounges and gymnasiums.

Pretty soon, maybe even bowling alleys and waterslides.

Where do you think you're going with THAT thing, Gary?

　　—I'm going on the airplane. It has a Slip-n-Slide. And a wading pool.

They won't let you carry that on the plane. You'll have to check it.

　—I don't want to check it. I like it. It looks like somebody I know.

I don't care who it looks like. You'll have to check it.

　　　—What will I use in the wading pool?

Use your seat cushion. It doubles as a flotation device.

—Fine.

So, which ticket would the average passenger purchase?

If the price is the same, Boeing believes he or she will choose A.

They don't think passengers care if there's a lounge bar on board. Or a bowling alley.

Passengers don't want to bowl. If it's a long flight, they probably want to sleep. And get to where they want to go . . . as quickly and efficiently and as comfortably as possible.

That's a job for the B787.

It's a competitive marketplace, though. And Airbus won't take the fight lying down.

So, to win passengers for the A380, their customers—the airlines—will have an opportunity to sell even *more* luxury perks, which, unfortunately, may make the plane heavier.

And less efficient.

Remember: This race goes to the swiftest *and* the most efficient.

And to be more cost efficient with the A380, *airlines need to fill planes*. And one time-tested way to fill planes is to sell more perks—perks that mean *less* space for passengers *and* possibly heavier aircraft, which mean *less* efficiency.

Not more.

Plus, things like bowling alleys and waterslides and whatever else they can think of will take up valuable seats—seats those airlines will need to sell to keep jumbo planes full of passengers, not amenities, *if* they want to make a profit.

At the moment, it could be a dicey proposition for Airbus, going up against the B787, a plane that can do things no other plane can do.

And it seems Boeing's strategy may fulfill another one of Clausewitz's dictums: "War is thus an act of force to compel our enemy to do our will."

(Lose, in other words.)

True. The B787 has about 49 percent less room than the A380.

It doesn't have a gym. And there aren't any *discothèques* on board.

But that doesn't matter—Boeing's *customer* strategy relies on the fact that today's airline passenger doesn't want to hang around doing traveling lunges—or Jell-O shots in traveling lounges—at 35,000 feet.

Did you bring a change of clothes for me?

　　　—I did. But I packed them.

Are they in the carry-on?

　　　—No. I checked them.

Then why did you let me work out?

　　　—You wanted to do some cardio before we made our final descent.

But I don't want to land in a sweaty shirt.

　　　—Wrap yourself in one of the bedsheets.

That's silly.

—Then go shirtless. No one will notice.

They want to go where they want to go.

Period.

The B787 can go farther than the A380.

It's more efficient per person.

And it takes passengers wherever they want to fly, without any layovers in Tokyo or Cairo or Mumbai.

The A380 can carry more people, but airlines need to keep those wheels up, and again, keep those big jumbo planes as full as possible to make any money.

Sure, they have cozy sleeper beds.

But they need to be priced relatively high to turn a profit.

Boeing believes that fast, direct flights—so fast there *might* not be time for a movie—and less crowded airplanes are nearest and dearest to the hearts of passengers.

They believe travelers still like having drinks served to them while sitting in comfy seats and don't necessarily want to stand in line and mingle at the "Mile-High" bar.

They'll be plenty of time for all that when they get to where they're going.

Where have you been?! I've been looking all over this plane for you!

—I was joining the Mile-High Club.

Why is your hair all messed up?

—I told you. I was joining the Mile-High Club.

What IS the Mile-High Club?

—The second rule of the Mile-High Club is you don't talk about the Mile-High Club.

Oh yeah? What's the first rule?

—No glass in the pool area.

At its core, Boeing's strategy relies on direct flights in a smaller, technologically innovative aircraft that's aesthetically pleasing and comfortable for today's passenger.

(The 787 offers plenty of headroom and better humidity levels because of the composite used to make the airplane.)

Boeing seems to be saying to its customers, This is what *technology* can do for you.

Airbus seems to be saying, This is what *bigness* can do for you.

In fact, Boeing has made *innovative* a synonym for *efficient*.

Where do they both stand now?

By early 2011, Boeing had nearly 850 orders for the B787 Dreamliners. Airbus had nearly 250 for the A380.

And the race goes on.

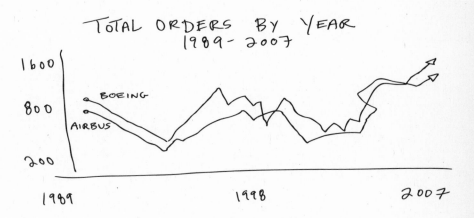

Source: http://www.smarttravelasia.com/AirbusVsBoeing.htm

Insights on their customers' customers—the passengers—fortified by lots of data helped Boeing make their decision to bet on the B787 strategy.

And what was Boeing's strategy, exactly?

Purpose: Make air travel as efficient and comfortable as possible for passengers . . . and as profitable as possible for their customers, the airlines.

Plan: Rather than rely on the ol' economies-through-scale bit, go for economy through innovation.

Series of actions: Invent a lighter, faster, high-tech plane that can fly farther, which will allow airlines to offer more point-to-point, or direct, flights to travelers who will then have more alternatives to the hub-and-spoke model.

Measurable goal: Deliver more airplanes than Airbus . . . and more happy customers, who want more airplanes.

And the narrative? Better. Not bigger.

There's an old rule in the airplane business.

—What's that?

Bigger is harder. The bigger airplanes become, the bigger the multipliers in the forces they need to overcome to stay in the air.

—How come?

It's a volume metric thing.

—What does THAT mean?

I THINK it means they need to be heavy to be strong. And that can be a problem when you want to fly.

—Just because you love
to fly doesn't mean you should be explaining aerodynamics.

Sometimes, though, hub and spoke is exactly what customers want.

Just maybe not airline customers.

Slava Rubin, one of the cofounders of indiegogo, chose the "hub-and-spoke" model when he and his partners needed to decide who they wanted to target in the marketplace: fundless folks looking to fund a cause . . . or funders looking for a cause to fund.

In the end, they decided it was less expensive and far more reasonable to develop a crowdfunding strategy to target the former.

"We started in 2008," Slava said, "when Google didn't own YouTube and Obama wasn't in office."

Before the BC to AD changeover, in other words.

The initial idea was to create a crowdfunding site that raised money for independent filmmakers.

Now, anybody can use indiegogo to raise money for any kind of cause.

"Just like Amazon, it was one vertical at first," Slava said. "Now, the sky is the limit."

—Amazon started as an online bookstore, didn't it, Larry?

I think so.

—Now it's "the world's largest online retailer," according to Wikipedia. They sell everything!

Not everything.

—Well. ALMOST everything.

They don't sell B787 Dreamliners.

—That's true. They don't. But I know where you can get a used Aeroflot Tupolev-104. It was owned by a nice little old man who only flew Moscow to Omsk to Irkutsk once a year.

I only fly Tupolev-124s or higher.

—Snob.

I Have a Strategy (No You Don't)

Focusing on user experience, simplicity, and customer happiness, Slava and his partners built a clean, easy-to-use crowdfunding site that uses a unique "gogofactor" algorithm to get the word out.

It's a free and open market on a free and open platform that treats everybody, not just "creatives," as equals.

It's part of the brand promise.

One has the power to seek funding for fertility treatments—for humans *or* pets.

Or a political cause.

Or a college education.

Anything, really, so long as it's legal.

I'm raising money for a new product, Gary!

—Really! What kind of product, Larry?

No, wait. It's a service.

—Oh. What kind of service?

One that will eradicate the need for ALL services!

—Is it a DIY model?

I think so. I'm having trouble reading my business plan.

—Maybe you should raise money for a LASIK operation first.

And what does winning look like?

"Being around a hundred years from now," Slava says.

For indiegogo, the strategy is clean, simple, and effective:

Purpose: Change the way the world gets funding.

Plan: Democratize the fund-raising process and allow people or "campaign owners" to find financial backing for just about anything.

Series of actions: Create open and accessible platform; develop powerful tools and a global reach; keep customers happy with a superior user experience, personalization, and lots of hand holding; respect and treat every funder equally.

Measurable goal: Last for at least one hundred years.

And the narrative?

Empowerment.

The strategy seems to be working.

The company now operates in 196 countries and boasts more than a hundred thousand campaigns.

In June 2012, it was reported that they received $15 million in venture capital to help get the start-up to scale and put the competition on the defensive.

Proof, perhaps, that the crowdfunder's children won't go shoeless.

Or fundless.

That's the upshot of a strategy for a start-up venture, a venture that has a moral obligation to earn a reasonable rate of return for investors.

What about ventures with different kinds of moral obligations, the ones that are after a social but not necessarily a financial return?

And how, exactly, is success measured when there aren't really metrics to measure the amount of good being done in the world other than business metrics?

—Business has taken over the business of saving the world, Larry.

How so, Gary?

—They have inflicted business metrics on nonprofits. They have imposed business language. Perhaps most damaging of all, ROI now determines who or what in this world needs saving. And when.

But you need business math to figure out whether medical professionals are making progress in the fight against a disease—like malaria, for example. Those answers will show whether the methods and treatments are working.

—Yes, but we should NOT rely on ROI to tell us that malaria is—or is not—a disease worth battling in the first place! That's absurd!

This feels like a fight. We better change the subject.

Good questions, to be sure.

And there aren't always easy answers.

Nonprofits are under all sorts of pressures these days—pressures that can't be relieved by simply bringing on another investor when they need more cash.

There are different pressures. And different rules.

Naturally, you need different strategies. Or, more accurately, strategies that are different, and that take into consideration the rules of giving and getting. Not buying and selling.

—Remember the good old days, before "buying" and "selling" replaced the artisan's idea of "work"?" And craft wasn't a dirty word?

Wait. There was a time BEFORE buying and selling?

—Yep.

I don't remember it, Gary.

—It was a long time ago, Larry. Before the rise of the labor market. Before everything was for sale.

But the sum of human happiness is defined by buying and selling, isn't it?

—I don't know. We don't seem to want to try anything else.

I have an idea! Write a book about a world beyond buying and selling and I'll publish it and we'll sell a million copies and make lots of money!

—See what I mean?

REDF in San Francisco has developed an interesting strategy for nonprofits.

The organization was started in 1997 by George R. Roberts to create all sorts of employment opportunities for the homeless.

According to a personal communication with Melinda Tuan, one of REDF's cofounders, the organization experimented with some different approaches to discover the best way to employ individuals who were homeless.

It partnered with government job training programs.

It partnered with other, like-minded social enterprises, too—nonprofits that were set up specifically to employ individuals, both young people and adults, with the biggest barriers and the highest hurdles in the job market.

It even tinkered with self-employment models.

Eventually, the folks behind REDF realized that self-employment was not a viable option. "Homeless people already have multiple barriers to employment," Tuan noted, "and needed more support in their endeavors."

REDF also learned that government programs impose too many time restrictions on homeless or recently homeless individuals who are seeking employment.

"The government programs were too time limited," Tuan added. "One cannot expect a homeless person to turn [his or her] life around in a thirty-, sixty-, or ninety-day period."

It took me years and years to become who I am.
I doubt that I'm going to change overnight, Gary!

—Don't fret. Overnight successes take a long time.
Sometimes decades. Just don't give up!

I won't. But I'm just letting you know, I can't change any faster than this.

—Incremental change. Isn't that what this is all about? Wait.
What IS this all about, anyway?

I'm trying to grow a mustache.

—This may take a while.

In the end, REDF decided to build a strategy to cooperate with social enterprises in the area that were running nonprofits with revenue-generating business models that already existed for the sole purpose of employing workers who would otherwise have little to no chance of being hired elsewhere.

These enterprises had a head start in the marketplace; they were already fighting the good fight; and they seemed to have the most potential for success: helping homeless learn the skills they needed to learn to find good, stable jobs . . . and keep them.

The strategy looked like this:

Purpose: Help homeless find jobs so they could find homes.

Plan: Supercharge nonprofits that were already running social enterprises to employ homeless, formerly homeless, and low-low-income individuals.

Series of actions: Develop business plans with nonprofits; fund business plans with operating grants, capital grants, recoverable grants, and so on; provide additional resources and services including financial management, board development, and evaluation consulting.

Measurable goal: For the individual, increase income in a stable job, find a home, and reduce reliance, for example, on food stamps. For the social enterprises, generate net income for parent nonprofit.

Narrative: An investment in employment *is* an investment in hope.

In 2012, REDF reported that to date it has supported fifty social enterprises that generated revenues of more than $115 million and successfully employed 6,500 people.

Not only that, REDF reported that 77 percent of social enterprise employees interviewed two years after they began their employment were still working. And average employee wages increased by 31 percent, and monthly incomes nearly doubled (90 percent).

Some things, of course, can't be measured. Nor should they be. Like the sense of accomplishment that one feels when one beats the odds. And the sense of pride and purpose one feels when one is happily and gainfully employed.

How do you measure happiness, Gary?

—Number of smiles.

And how do you count love?

—By the price of birthday gifts, I suppose.

AHA! So you DIDN'T forget to remove the price tag! You knew it was there all along!

—I'm going to start answering the questions I wish I were asked.

Still, REDF has plenty of tangible, measurable results for those who are compelled to "count" success. Like jobs acquired, jobs retained. Wages earned, wages increased.

Not to mention the decreased costs of homelessness and joblessness.

It certainly pays to give, in more ways than one.

What do you want to do in the world, Gary?

—I think the question is, What do
I want to do FOR the world, Larry?

What do you want to do FOR it, then?

—I want to change the world.

To what?

—I don't know.

Why do you want to change it, then?

—I'm restless. I'm bored.
And I'm frightened of boredom.

Sounds like YOU need a change. Not the world.

Here's another example of a strategy in action, one that was used to create an entirely new concept in education and challenge the very idea of what a school should be.

It's the story of the Academy for Global Citizenship (AGC), a public charter school on Chicago's southwest side.

A school quite unlike any other school in the city.

Maybe the country.

With an emphasis on "transdisciplinary education," AGC meets the physical, emotional, cultural, and social needs of the student.

And prepares them to adjust, adapt, and learn in a world where change is the only constant.

The school is grounded in the principals of environmental stewardship. Students learn in green classrooms and are assigned jobs with such titles as "recycling director" and "vermicompost bin manager."

I hated school.

I used to get beat up.

Did you get beat up?

—No. I was very popular.

I was popular, too . . . with the kids who wanted to beat me up.

Much better than being "hall monitor."

Students learn about the environment and how to live in harmony with it in a lush, schoolyard garden with all sorts of plants and vegetables. And chickens.

They learn about good nutrition and the importance of healthy eating as it relates to the whole body: mind, spirit, everything.

We are what we eat, after all.

There's meditation. There's yoga. There's relationship building.

Through it all, kids learn how to read and write, and all the other things they need to learn to be conscientious and productive global citizens.

And from a deeply collaborative relationship with teachers, parents, and the entire community, a smarter, empathetic, and more socially and environmentally aware student emerges.

Yoga helps me calm down and think clearly, Gary.

—You should be careful with that kind of stuff.

Why?

—Clarity of vision breeds its own kind of madness with you.

Who told you that?

—You did.

Must have been right after some really hot yoga.

The battle has been all uphill for Sarah Elizabeth Ippel, who was just twenty-three years old when she first appeared before the board of education and asked members to reimagine schools with her.

Some told her it couldn't be done.

Some said reforming the system within the system was impossible.

Some believed you couldn't reform the reformers—and they were the ones who needed the most help, since they couldn't seem to get out of their own way.

She proved everybody wrong. Mostly by making "reform" a human issue, not a human capital issue.

Should children be turned into ANY form of capital, human or otherwise?

—I don't think so, Larry.

Then why are education reformers so hung up on human capital?

—Because nobody has bothered to frame the conversation or the problem in a different way.

Maybe we should do that.

—Maybe we should. You go first.

I got nothing.

—Thinking beyond what you know is tough, isn't it?

I still got nothing.

—Don't worry. It will come. Pay attention to your breathing.

Now in its fourth year, the AGC is succeeding beyond all expectations.

When she began this journey, Sarah Elizabeth just wanted to create an extraordinary learning community in one of Chicago's underserved neighborhoods.

Her goal now is nothing short of reimagining the world of public education.

"The purpose has changed and grown over these past few years in response to the challenges and complexities that exist within the school system," she says. "Simply put, we're out to transform the way not just our city, but the entire nation, sees and understands what's possible in education."

Sure. There have been mistakes along the way. But, Sarah Elizabeth says, part of her success has been to identify those glitches as they occur, in real time, course-correcting as needed.

"I started the school when I was twenty-three, and, let's face it, I didn't really know a lot about public education."

She has been actively managing her strategy over the years, tweaking and refining aspects as needed . . . even the goal.

Initially, she wanted to replicate the entire model throughout the school system.

Now, however, she intends to reproduce only the parts that appear to be working.

—Obest plerumque iis qui discere volunt authoritas eorum qui docent!

What does THAT mean?

—"For those who want to learn, the obstacle can often be the authority of those who teach!"

Who said THAT?

—Montaigne, quoting Erasmus, after Cicero.

Who are THOSE people?

—You didn't learn about them when you were getting your MBA, did you?

No.

—That's a shame. You'd probably be twice as dangerous in the business world if you did.

I want a refund.

"We're thinking every day about how to identify and refine strands of the school's model and replicate them in a way that will have an immediate impact on four to five hundred kids in Chicago public schools," Sarah Elizabeth said.

"And do it *tomorrow*."

These days, a bulk of her efforts are devoted to engagement: Engaging teachers, parents, and board members; engaging the political, legal, and education communities; engaging her counterparts at the school, making sure each group is aligned with the vision and understands how it will be realized.

Most important, they must know how success will be measured. Right now, it's simple math:

"We want to ignite a movement that will positively affect 20 million students by 2020," she said.

To do this, AGC needs support from various constituencies.

And a sense of *belief*.

"People need to believe that they can do anything. Once they believe they can do anything, they will believe that they can create a better world and understand their role in that world."

To believe, you need to forget how to doubt.

—And if you forget how to doubt,
then what happens?
Do you believe?

Yes. And when you believe, you forget how to lose.
And you know who THAT makes you?

—Martina Navratilova?

I was thinking more Bobby Riggs.

—What if I wear lifts? Will that help?

Maybe.

AGC's strategy at a glance:

Purpose: Reimagine what's possible in public education.

Plan: Create an extraordinary learning community in a school or lab environment; extract and scale the elements that are working.

Series of actions: Develop strategic relationships on local and national levels; leverage and utilize relationships to navigate political waters; simultaneously engage other hyper-local groups and communities to maintain positivity, boost morale, and promote school's broader impact on society; replicate and implement successful modular innovations.

Measurable goal: Positively affect 20 million kids by 2020.

She has a unique and effective model, parts of which can be easily replicated in school districts everywhere.

And a grand strategy to implement it.

Plus, she has a great story to tell.

School doesn't need to be just another investment in human capital.

It doesn't really need to be "school" at all.

School can become the birthplace of the global citizen.

Okay, Gary, I think I got this strategy thing down. If we do A, then B will happen, which results in C! Got it?

—People won't get it until you spontaneously draw a Cartesian quadrant graph on a dry erase board during a meeting . . . while wearing a Cartesian-era hat!

I want to draw one. Believe me, I want to. But I can never find a marker with ink in it around this place.

And we all of us have the power to make it happen.

It's a narrative that can be summed up in one word:

Believe!

Funny thing about narratives, Gary.

        —What's that?

They don't map to ends. They ACHIEVE them.

        —What do you mean?

Think of the people who run for president.
Their narratives are usually about progress
and prosperity, but their ends are always
about 50 percent of the vote PLUS one.

        —I don't see the connection.

I don't think there is one.

        —I think I'm ready for a new narrative.

You'll have to wait until election year.

        —Oh.

Now that you know the elements of strategy, you should feel more confident about what you do (and how you do it) the next time you do it.

I have a new strategy, Gary,
but I don't have a reason to use it.

—That's like having a cure
without a disease, Larry.

Will you create a disease so I can
cure it with my strategy?

—Why?

That's how I pay my light bill.

—You should develop a strategy that
doesn't require you to rely on electricity.

Are you suggesting that I just think in the dark?

—You mean you don't already?

Just make sure you know what winning looks like, which is something that will be determined by *you* . . . *not* your strategy.

I don't know what I want, Gary.

—Then teach yourself what to want, Larry.

I think I want to be loved, Gary.

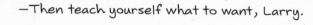

—You have to love to be loved, Larry.

Oh. Then maybe I'll do something else. Maybe I'll focus on being LIKED.

—Well, that's better than starting a holy war.

Once you know your goal—and how to measure your success—you just need to figure out the best, most efficient way to achieve it.

And the best way to tell your story.

What's wrong, Gary?

—I don't know if I should sing my narrative, dance my narrative, or mime my narrative.

I think you should just impose the will of your narrative on the people through every available channel and force them to accept your assessment of the world and everything in it. And if anybody contradicts you and your ideas, then the majority of your brand loyalists will do your dirty work and make dissenting consumers feel silly, out of touch, and low class.

—That makes me a dictator, doesn't it?

No. I think it makes you Apple.

Understanding the elements of strategy should help.

A lot.

Knowing what *strategy* means—and *doesn't* mean—should help, too.

—You know, culture EATS strategy
for lunch. And culture is nothing if
not character, Gary. And
character is fate.

What makes you say that?

—If people are not happy or valued in
a culture, they won't care a lick
about strategy. Other than the
strategy to escape the culture.

And?

—If people are happy and valued in a culture,
and there's a transcendent interest for the
group, they will actually live and BREATHE
strategy. And they will achieve anything.

So?

—I'm just saying, culture
EATS strategy for lunch.

You're not saying. You're repeating.

—You're right. I'll save that culture bit for
another book.

I Have a Strategy (No You Don't)

Whatever you do from now on, please don't ever use a word in a conversation *if* you do not know what the word means.

And if you *think* you know what it means, check before you use the word.

Just to be sure.

Especially the word *strategy*.

Especially if you're doing the talking. And you're the only person in the room.

That would mean you're probably an MBA.

And you're crazy.

And you really shouldn't be both.

The End (which is really The Beginning).

Didn't Heraclitus say that?

—People SAY he said it. But who knows?

Can't argue with "Who knows?"

—Yes. I can.

I really hate you.

—What's hate but
an imperfect
form of love?

No. I'm pretty sure it's just hate.

—I love you, anyway, Larry.

PRINCIPAL SOURCES

Clausewitz, Carl von. *On War,* originally *Vom Kriege.* Edited and translated by Michael Howard and Peter Paret. Princeton University Press, 1984.

David Kotz with Fred Weir. *Revolution from Above: The Demise of the Soviet System.* New York: Routledge, 1997.

Montaigne, Michel de. *The Complete Essays,* translated and edited by M. A. Screech. Penguin Books, 2003.

Ramo, Joshua Cooper. *The Age of the Unthinkable.* Little, Brown and Company, 2009.

http://aeroweekly.blogspot.com/2010/08/boeing-787-dreamliner-vs-airbus-a380.html

http://blogs.wsj.com/venturecapital/2012/06/06/the-daily-start-up-indiegogo-joins-crowd-with-15m-series-a/

http://classics.mit.edu/Tzu/artwar.html

http://www.agcchicago.org/roots.php

http://www.dailyfinance.com/2012/07/17/boeing-sales-discount-airplanes

http://www.forbes.com/2006/05/23/unsolicited-advice-advertising-cx_meb_0524boeing.html

http://www.indiegogo.com

http://online.wsj.com/article/SB10001424052748703513604575310622939329664.html

http://www.redf.org

http://www.smarttravelasia.com/AirbusVsBoeing.htm

http://en.wikipedia.org/wiki/Aeroflot

http://en.wikipedia.org/wiki/Amazon.com

http://en.wikipedia.org/wiki/Clausewitz

http://en.wikipedia.org/wiki/Military_strategy

Howell J. Malham Jr. is cofounder and director of Insight Labs, a humanitarian foundation that convenes the smartest, most influential people to tackle the world's toughest problems.

A recovering brand strategist, Howell has worked with a number of prominent companies including Walgreens, Allstate, Universal Studios, LEGO, and HarperCollins. He has also written for the *New York Times*, the *Los Angeles Times*, and the *Chicago Tribune*.

Howell has been drawing and painting his entire life. His illustrations have played a supporting role in his work as a strategist and a writer over the years.

He lives in Chicago with his wife, Cheryl.